A Man Named Saul

True Story

Paul Ekroth

A Man Named Saul

True Story

Published by Lucid Books in Houston, TX
www.LucidBooks.com

ISBN: 978-1-63296-651-3
eISBN: 978-1-63296-619-3

Special Sales: Most Lucid Books titles are available in special quantity discounts. Custom imprinting or excerpting can also be done to fit special needs. Contact Lucid Books at Info@LucidBooks.com

Table of Contents

Introduction

Saul was a bona fide believer, a devoted follower of Judaism. Born in a province ruled and controlled by Ancient Rome, Saul's father was a man of wealth and success. As a result, he and his family were granted the honor of becoming Roman citizens. Saul was born a Roman citizen.

As a young man, Saul began to hear gossip about a man in Jerusalem who was said to perform miracles. Jesus was not sanctioned by the synagogue, yet his influence was a major threat to Judaism. Attendance was down while thousands were flocking to hear this man who claimed to be the Son of God! "This man Jesus, is an imposter who is practicing fakery," claimed Saul, "It must be stopped!"

Saul thought, "Fortunately, good sense prevailed, and Jesus was put to death." Then Saul heard bad news. The followers of this supposedly dead Jesus were still active, and the worst was yet to come! The followers of Jesus were multiplying, and Saul believed that it had become worse than it was while Jesus walked the streets of Jerusalem! Saul felt that it was his duty and God's will that he would end this travesty of following a dead man, named Jesus. First, he had to obtain legal authority from the High Priest to bind, hold, and imprison all who are followers of this Jesus—both men and women.

With a number of strong-armed men, Saul began his task to serve God by cleansing the earth from this fallacy. On the road to Damascus, as they were walking, a bright light flashed from the sky. It was so bright and forceful that Saul and his men collapsed helplessly onto the ground. Blinded by the light and with their strength totally depleted, Saul's companions lay there as dead men unaware of the event occurring directly beside them. Jesus appeared to Saul and said, "Saul, Saul, why are you persecuting me" (Acts 9:4)? No one but Saul could see Jesus or hear the words spoken. Within a few moments, Saul was transformed into a new man.

From the creation of Adam to Saul, humans existed on earth for approximately five thousand years. Throughout those years, forty biblical authors wrote about their lives and experiences, but only one author wrote on all biblical subjects, from creation to the rapture of the Church. He wrote on subjects about which Christians still struggle to understand and agree. He wrote more in regard to Christian doctrine than any other human. His birth name was Saul, but he is best known as the Apostle Paul!

Chapter 1

There's a New Boy in Town

Fifteen hundred years passed from the day that Moses led God's suffering people, the Israelites, out of Egypt from their captivity. All those years later, a faint cry broke the silence with the birth of a baby boy. Belonging to the tribe of Benjamin, the infant was named in honor of Israel's first king, Saul.

Saul was born in Tarsus, a region of Cilicia, during the years that Rome dominated many nations. Saul's parents had wealth and because they lived in Tarsus, they were given the honor of being citizens of Rome. As a result, Saul was born a Roman citizen, although he was a Hebrew (Acts 16:37, 22:25–29).

Saul's Education

Saul was taught the traditions of the fathers from early childhood. Jewish law prescribed that a boy began the study of the Scriptures at age five, and the study of the legal traditions at age ten. His native language was Greek, but Saul's residence, later in Palestine, gave him knowledge of the Syrian Chaldean languages of the day. Jewish education sought to produce a man who could both think and act. An early Jewish counsel states, "Whosoever doth not teach his son work, teacheth him to rob!"[1] At age thirteen, a Jewish boy became a "bar mitzvah," the "son of commandment," at which time he took upon himself the full obligation of the Law. The most promising lads were directed to rabbinic school to study under able teachers. When Saul was about fourteen years of age, he was sent to Jerusalem to study under the greatest rabbi of the first century: Gamaliel.

Educated according to the strict manner of the Law from the fathers, Saul was amongst the elite of his day. The Law of Moses was stamped into Saul's memory. He learned right from wrong and was determined to abide by the Law as given by God to Moses.

It's a New Day

Saul was born at a very unusual moment in world history. No one could conceive of a day when God would rearrange the ancient order of events given to Moses so very long ago. People believed that any attempt to cause a change was blasphemous against God and all who are righteous. They believed that anyone who opposed the written law despised God and was unworthy of life. Moses was God's messenger, and each person had the responsibility not just to obey, but to enforce law and order, as stated in Law. Not to do so was blasphemous against God, Moses, and all morality (Leviticus 24:10–23, Numbers 15:17–36).

While in Jerusalem, Saul heard "whispering" that Jesus "who they crucified" was alive! Even more amazing, he found that people were worshiping Jesus as if he was God. Saul, a young man of integrity and determination, felt the responsibility to stop those imposters who were

1. Robert Young, Young's Analytical Concordance to the Bible: Paul (Peabody, MA: Hendrickson Academic, 1998), 735.

endeavoring to substitute God's holy law with the teaching of a carpenter who had mastered the practice of trickery.

Saul sincerely believed that the Jesus crowd was deceived and up to no good. The Old Testament states that those guilty of violating any one of the Ten Commandments were worthy of death. Saul, willing to obey God's law, would do his very best to honor God, by ending this travesty caused by one known as Jesus who no longer was alive.

Saul became relentless in his pursuit to stop the growth of Christianity. In agreement with the Jewish leaders, Saul was given the authority to enforce the laws of Judaism on all Jews, both men and women. Under Saul's authority, people who believed in Jesus were dragged from their homes (Acts 8:3).]

The First Christian Martyr

Stephen, a Jew, was so convinced that Jesus was truly the Christ sent from God that he stood on a street corner, proclaiming that Jesus had come from heaven to redeem all who believed in God. People began to gather; Saul was there also. As Stephen's sermon continued, people became angry—so angry that many wished Stephen was dead. Saul was in full agreement that Stephen should die. Saul held the robes of the mob as they stoned Stephen until he was dead (Acts 7:58–60, 8:3).

Power Hungry

Regardless of Saul's authority, his desire for greater authority and power continued to increase. Breathing threats and murder against all who believed in this Jesus, Saul requested additional help from the Synagogue. Finally, Saul received a letter signed by the High Priest granting him authority to bind and confine both men and women who follow the teachings of this Jesus.

In Jerusalem, Saul imprisoned many who believed in Jesus. Having authority from the chief priests, Saul with some strong-armed men, would venture into surrounding cities, beginning with Damascus. Should Saul find any belonging to "The Way," they would be removed from their home and taken to prison and possibly beaten. Some were killed according to Saul's own words! Believers in Jesus are known as Christians, but in Paul's day, they were called "People of the Way" (Acts 8:3; 9:2; 26:10–11).

Chapter 2
Saul's Transformation

Due to Saul's upbringing, he could have succeeded in any occupation that he desired. Working with his hands provided a living, not satisfaction.

Saul could have easily become a priest. However, a priest must act priestly, but priestly was not a part of Saul's agenda. Instead, Saul desired to be "God's lightening rod" to discipline those who disobeyed the law of God. Having received the authority he desired, Saul and his men were on their way to Damascus when a light burst on them (Acts 9:1–2, 3–9; 26:10–11, 12–14). The light was brighter than the sun, and the burst of light caused Saul and his men to collapse helplessly to the ground.

Saul Met Jesus

On the ground and unable to rise, they all heard a voice that spoke to Saul; yet no one was visible. The voice said:

He heard a voice saying to him, "Saul, Saul, why are you persecuting me?" And he said, "Who are you, Lord?" And he said, "I am Jesus, whom you are persecuting. But rise and enter the city, and you will be told what you are to do."

—Acts 9:4–6 (cf. Acts 26:14–15)

The men who were with Saul became frightened to the extent that they became speechless. Able to hear the voice but unable to see anyone, Saul eventually stood and opened his eyes, but he could see nothing. Saul had become blind. The men took Saul by the hand and led him into Damascus to the street named Straight where they found the house occupied by a man named Judas. For three days, Saul remained in the house; he was blind and refused to eat or drink (Acts 9:7–8).

Now in Damascus, lived a man named Ananias, a disciple of Christ:

The Lord said to him in a vision, "Ananias." And he said, "Here I am, Lord." And the Lord said to him, "Rise and go to the street called Straight, and at the house of Judas look for a man of Tarsus named Saul, for behold, he is praying, and he has seen in a vision a man named Ananias come in and lay his hands on him so that he might regain his sight." But Ananias answered, "Lord, I have heard from many about this man, how much evil he has done to your saints at Jerusalem. And here he has authority from the chief priests to bind all who call on your name." But the Lord said to him, "Go, for he is a chosen instrument of mine to carry my name before the Gentiles and kings and the children of Israel. For I will show him how much he must suffer for the sake of my name."

—Acts 9:10–16

> *So Ananias departed and entered the house. And laying his hands on him he said, "Brother Saul, the Lord Jesus who appeared to you on the road by which you came has sent me so that you may regain your sight and be filled with the Holy Spirit."*
>
> **—Acts 9:17**

Immediately, as Ananias placed his hands on Saul, something like "scales" fell from Saul's eyes, and he was able to see. Having regained his sight, Saul was "filled with the Holy Spirit." He was baptized in water; then he ate food and was strengthened.

A Lesson Learned

Saul, the son of religious parents, was taught the difference between right and wrong. He was well informed about the covenant that God gave to Moses. Saul believed that those who violated any one of those laws deserved death (Leviticus 24:10–23; Numbers 15:17–36).

Saul was taught that priests were appointed by God and that they spoke on God's behalf. Those who would like to know God's purpose for their life should ask a priest. Saul would soon discover that all humans, priests included, sometimes have their own agenda.

Pride and authority can be an addiction difficult to control. Though appointed by God, many priests failed to recognize the words of the Prophets, who repeatedly prophesized that a permanent sacrifice would, one day, replace the yearly temporal sacrifice. The death of Christ ended the yearly animal sacrifice. There has been no animal sacrifice since the death of Christ.

Saul's discovery of Christ revolutionized his life. Prior to this encounter, Saul had believed that he knew all that there was to know about God and his holy prophets. When Ananias placed his hands on Saul, the blindness left immediately, and Saul was filled with the Holy Spirit. Before he met

Jesus, Saul had waged a religious war on God's behalf, attempting to rid the world of Christianity. Jesus chose Saul to spread the Jesus message beyond Jerusalem and into the entire world.

Saul was intellectual and a religious man who followed the dictates of his heart as he believed them to be. It required the strange happening on the road to Damascus to change his long held views and set him on a different course.

Saul, the Missionary

Saul became the first evangelist to spread the gospel message to nations beyond Jerusalem. Saul proclaimed the gospel for the first time in Antioch, Eastern parts of Asia Minor, Philippi, Athens, Corinth, Ephesus, and distant nations of that time. With zeal, Saul had tried to end Christianity; he now used that same zeal to promote the gospel of Jesus Christ.

For the first time, Saul realized that we are all children of Adam, created by God. As a result of God's creation, He alone established the rules. God's love extends to all people, not just a few. It is God's will that no man should perish; yet we perish as a result of our unwillingness to honor the Almighty who created us. We become chosen by God through our obedience and as result we may live forever.

Old Testament Logic

It was Saul's critical examination of the Old Testament that drove him to understand spiritual mysteries that had existed for several thousand years, but were not fully understood. Suddenly, the Scriptures came alive to Saul after he had received the Holy Spirit.

Chapter 3
A New Earth

The Lord God formed the man of dust from the ground and breathed into his nostrils the breath of life, and the man became a living creature.

—Genesis 2:7

The Lord God caused a deep sleep to fall upon the man, and while he slept took one of his ribs and closed up its place with flesh. And the rib that the Lord God had taken from the man he made into a woman.

—Genesis 2:21–22

It was in the beginning that God created the heavens and the earth. When earth's beginning occurred remains unknown. Neither are we fully aware of the first earth's appearance. We do know, as stated in Genesis, that the earth lost its appearance, becoming formless and empty.

Before God created human life, He created all the other creatures, saying:

- "Let the waters swarm with swarms of living creatures" (Genesis 1:20).
- "Let birds fly above the earth across the expanse of the heavens" (Genesis 1:20).
- "Let the earth bring forth living creatures according to their kinds" (Genesis 1:24).

The creature kingdom breathed on their own.

When God made man, He said, *"Let us make man in our image, after our likeness. And let them have dominion over the fish of the sea and over the birds of the heavens and over the livestock and over all the earth"* (Genesis 1:26). No creature received the breath of God; all the creatures breathed on their own. Man was very different from every creature. He was to rule over the animal kingdom, as if he were God.

Only humanity was made in God's likeliness, and only humanity was given the breath of God, so that all humanity would live forever. The human body was made of earth, to which the body will return. The breath of God is the soul everlasting, and only God is able to end His life. Animals do not have God's breath. When they die, it's over. Humans live on after the body has returned to the earth; we live without the body forever. Only God can end His breath if He chooses.

It is believed that four substances are required for life to exist on earth: soil, air, heat, and water. Without the sun's fire, no life could exist on earth. Remove the water and air from the earth, and this planet would join the celestial lifeless planets, wandering in the sky. One of earth's most important essentials is its soil.

Soil

Only the material contained in earth's soil allows life to exist on earth. It is the "earth" that contains the components required by plants to exist, and cattle exist from the plants. "Meat-eaters" live due to the cattle that eat the plants. All medicines, vitamins, and food are products produced from the soil. From wood to the fish that swim on the bottom of the sea to the birds that nest high in the hills—all are products of the earth.

Earth is so mysterious that experts are unable to duplicate the mysterious elements concealed within the earth. It was God who used earth to create Adam. God formed a body for Adam, but that body had no life until God breathed into Adam's nostrils and Adam became a living soul. God then caused Adam to sleep, and as he slept, God removed a rib from Adam's side and closed the flesh as though nothing had happened.

God made Eve. Adam likely witnessed the entire process as a dream as he slept. If not, we would not know the facts. The story teaches us that all life begins in the male, yet only the female has the capacity to reproduce that life into its own kind.

Lucifer was one of God's holy angels. God appointed Lucifer with the authority to watch and protect earth; Lucifer had a large number of angels under his command who supported him. The idea that Lucifer and his angels all became devils on their journey from heaven to earth is not believable. It is more likely that something happened long before the Genesis account that caused Lucifer to become the devil and his angels to become demons.

Bible scholars have placed Adam at approximately 4004 BC. They arrived at earth's age by counting the age of the biblical characters and adding the few days required to explain what God had created. Geologists who have studied the earth believe the earth to be very old. In fact, geologists claim that around 4000 BC, the earth was recovering from an ice age that had devastated the earth. If that is so, that is in full agreement with my book (Creations Story[2]), which asserts that God destroyed the first earth with a flood, which was so devastating that the sun's radiation was unable to penetrate the dense moisture that lifted the water below. The water covered the entire earth to a depth that covered earth's highest mountains. Without the sun's radiant heat, brutal cold settled in, and the atmosphere became so cold that even the oceans froze, killing all sea life. Earth became as cold as the distant planets; the earth became a ball of ice.

Fortunately, creatures that had wandered the earth left proof that they had once existed as their skeletal remains were discovered throughout the earth.

Genesis 1:2 tells us that earth had become void, empty of life, and in total darkness, submerged beneath water. It was in the very beginning that God created a heaven and an earth, not a heaven and a body of water.

---

2. Paul Ekroth, Creations Story: Historical, Scientific, Biblical (Meadville, PA: Christian Faith Publishing, Inc, 2028).

Chapter 4
Adam and Eve

God's first appearance was to Adam, the father of all humanity. This event occurred some four thousand years prior to the birth of Saul. The earth, at that time, was perfect in every aspect. The massive oceans were nonexistent. Weeds, poison ivy, and other troublesome plants were not in existence. There were no insects, no dangerous creatures, and even the bee was friendly. The food supply was without end. Weather was constantly ideal, and humanity could not become sick or die since neither death nor sickness existed.

God told Adam that the entire earth was for human pleasure—except for one item: a tree that stood in the center of the garden. The tree was luxurious in appearance with mouthwatering fruit hanging from its branches. Being in the garden's center, the tree was on constant display, a reminder that choice is constant and always probing. The name of the tree was "knowledge of good and evil," and God said, "For in the day that you eat of it you shall surely die." (Genesis 2:17).

God's first appearance was to Adam, the father of all humanity. This event occurred some four thousand years prior to the birth of Saul. The earth, at that time, was perfect in every aspect. The massive oceans were nonexistent. Weeds, poison ivy, and other troublesome plants were not in existence. There were no insects, no dangerous creatures, and even the bee was friendly. The food supply was without end. Weather was constantly ideal, and humanity could not become sick or die since neither death nor sickness existed.

God told Adam that the entire earth was for human pleasure—except for one item: a tree that stood in the center of the garden. The tree was luxurious in appearance with mouthwatering fruit hanging from its branches. Being in the garden's center, the tree was on constant display, a reminder that choice is constant and always probing. The name of the tree was "knowledge of good and evil," and God said, "For in the day that you eat of it you shall surely die." (Genesis 2:17).

The Forbidden Tree

The earth was alive with many trees, but because God had said, "not that tree," that tree became the center of attraction. Why not that tree? Was it so alluring that God wanted it all for Himself? That was the thinking that elevated that tree above all other trees. No one was able to discover true happiness unless they sampled the fruit of the forbidden tree, or so they thought.

Of all the bad luck, God saw Adam and Eve eat from the forbidden tree. Adam and Eve heard the sound of God walking in the garden. They hid in the bushes in remorse for their disobedience, and God played their little game of hide and seek by asking, "Where are you" (Genesis 3:9)? All our wrongs are performed directly in God's view. God sees all our bad deeds, and he also sees the good that we do. God sees and knows all things at all times, whether night or day. God is always in the unseen present.

The Cost of Sin

Adam had the choice of seeking instant gratification by eating the fruit of the tree or living forever in obedience to God. As a result of Adam's bad judgement, sin was followed by death, and that became the inheritance of all Adam's children, which we are. Even the ground became cursed, producing weeds and thorns, rather than food.

"By the sweat of your face you shall eat bread, till you return to the ground, for out of it you were taken; for you are dust, and to dust you shall return" (Genesis 3:19), said the Creator. Animals became wild, and the weather became unpredictable. To Eve, God added new sorrows connected with childbearing. Adam listened to Eve rather than God; as a result, we all reap the consequence of death for their disobedience.

God had said, "The day you eat [of that tree] you shall surely die" (Genesis 2:17). That same day they lost their eternal existence, and the death process began. Like Adam and Eve, all humans are destined to die. We, the descendants of Adam, have inherited Adam's corrupt nature, desiring to do as we please. Saul quoted the psalmist who said, "None is righteous, no, not one" (Romans 3:10; cf., Psalm 14:3).

With His death on the cross, Jesus, who was without sin, died in Adam's stead. Because a perfect man died in Adam's stead, we the offspring of Adam have the perfect sacrifice to free us from the penalty of death. Sin came from one man and infected all mankind. The death of one holy man justified all who by faith receive Christ. I should have died, but Jesus died in my place. Because Adam is the father of all mankind, we also must die. However, in Christ, we can live again regardless of the fact that the body dissolves back into the earth, from which it came. Everlasting life is God's gift to all who truly repent. Jesus said, "Everyone who lives and believes in me shall never die" (John 11:26). This means that this body made from earth will be replaced with an everlasting body created by God.

After Adam and Eve sinned, God killed an animal, removed its skin, and used that skin to make garments for Adam and Eve for they were naked. The purpose of the animal's death was not to hide their nudity; rather the animal skin was used to hide their spiritual nakedness: they had become contaminated by sin. The death of the animal provided a cover for sin, but not total forgiveness. They still died. The moment Adam and Eve ate the fruit from that tree, a strange thing happened in their bodies: the death process began, and suddenly they realized that they were naked. Birds had feathers; animals had fur to cover their bodies; fish had scales, but humans were naked. In shame they hid themselves among the trees.

Chapter 5

Infinite Knowledge

Man has access to historical knowledge of the past as well as knowledge of today. Tomorrow is filled with uncertainty. God knows tomorrow as if it had occurred yesterday. The Old and New Testaments reveal God as knowing future events as authentically as if the events had just occurred. There is nothing that has occurred or will occur that God has not previously known. How God knows all events even thousands of years in advance is a mystery that is unexplainable.

The word of God came to the prophet Jeremiah stating:

> *"Before I formed you in the womb I knew you, and before you were born I consecrated you; I appointed you a prophet to the nations." Then I said, "Ah, Lord God! Behold, I do not know how to speak, for I am only a youth." But the Lord said to me, "Do not say, 'I am only a youth'; for to all to whom I send you, you shall go, and whatever I command you, you shall speak."*
>
> **—Jeremiah 1:4–7**

David wrote, "The steps of a man are established by the Lord, when he delights in his way; though he fall, he shall not be cast headlong, for the Lord upholds his hand" (Psalm 37:23–24). Then David added, "I have been young, and now am old, yet I have not seen the righteous forsaken or his children begging for bread" (Psalm 37:25).

God's presence is throughout the universe—an invisible spirit that cannot be detected or seen, even by angels, unless granted by God. We are able to detect the air we breathe; yet the invisible God cannot be detected. He who had no beginning is real. Although He is undetectable, He covers the entire earth with His presence, continually.

The psalmist said that no one can depart from God's presence:

> *O Lord, you have searched me and known me! You know when I sit down and when I rise up; you discern my thoughts from afar. You search out my path and my lying down and are acquainted with all my ways. . . . Where shall I go from your Spirit? Or where shall I flee from your presence? If I ascend to heaven, you are there! If I make my bed in Sheol, you are there! If I take the wings of the morning and dwell in the uttermost parts of the sea, even there your hand shall lead me.*
>
> **—Psalm 139:1–3, 7–9**

Because God fills the earth and the entire universe, there are no hidden secrets. Not only is God in the present, but His eye is also on each object in the universe. He even sees when a sparrow falls to the ground. He knows the number of hairs on each human's head. As we pray to God, whether silently or out loud, God hears our prayer—loud and clear. There are no mysteries, no secret thoughts, nothing hidden from God. He knows the depth of our thoughts with more honesty and accuracy than we (Matthew 10:29–30).

Chapter 6

The Naked Truth

God planted the tree of knowledge in the Garden of Eden, knowing that one day, humans would eat its fruit! God knew that Lucifer would attempt to deceive Eve into eating fruit from the forbidden tree. God allowed Satan to exist on earth. God, who has absolute power over the entire universe, simply could have dissolved the devil along with his fallen angels or confined them on a distant planet. But God chose not to do so. Together with a cursed earth, God added a group of fallen angels, known as demons, and their boss, Lucifer, the devil.

Among those seasoned characters, God placed two very innocent persons who had never seen death, nor had Eve ever spoken to God. Neither Eve nor Adam was advised that there was a devil in the garden. There were mysteries associated with life that God never acquainted them with. Who knew that a trickster also lived in the garden?

Job

The book of Job is the story of a sincere man who attempted to please God in every aspect of life; yet Job became plagued with painful boils from the top of his head to the bottom of his feet. In addition to the boils, Job suffered lost when a group of bandits raided his property and stole all his cattle. As Job was lying on the ground, filled with a painful affliction, his seven sons and three daughters were at a feast eating and drinking; suddenly a great wind came across the wilderness and struck the house. All Job's children died in the house, and only one servant escaped to tell Job.

Job's wife, hearing of the news, came to Job and said (in a manner of speaking), "So you still believe in God? Why don't you curse God and die" (Job 2:9)? Job replied that her words were foolish, spoken out of her emotions rather than her intellect. Job than inquired, "Shall we receive good from God, and shall we not receive evil" (Job 2:10)?

Job had been a very wealthy man until these destructive events left him a poor man. The trouble reminded Job that he was not fully in charge. There was one greater than he, who was able to take or give wealth. Job passed the test, and the Lord blessed Job's latter days more than in his beginning. Job's life ended with him having "14,000 sheep, 6,000 camels, 1,000 yoke of oxen, and 1,000 female donkeys" (Job 42:12). Job remarried, became the father of seven new sons and three daughters, lived to the age of 140. What became of Job's first wife is not stated.

The Struggle

The food garden has no value until the product is removed from the garden. The apple has no value unless it is removed from the tree. The professional prize fighter cannot succeed unless he exerts his physical body beyond its natural limits. Physical strength requires willingness to labor in the attempt to achieve satisfaction.

Adam was required to work. Eve, without required work, became mischievous. To be happy, humans are required to assume responsibility and to work. God made the universe and created humans in His likeness; therefore, we require work to be content (Genesis 1:26).

Is God Fair?

When an act is completed, we then judge: was it good, or was it bad? Adam, the father of all humanity, corrupted the human race by his disobedience. If we were born without sin, we would not die. The infant has not sinned and is at peace with God (Matthew 19:14; Mark 10:14).

At the age of accountability, Adam's rebellious nature becomes obvious. With age the child rebels against authority. Adam was offered the gift of everlasting life, but he rejected that for a bite of what was forbidden. That rebellious nature presents itself in all humanity. Is God fair in His judgments? God created each living object in the universe. Should He not demand some sort of order to His most choice creation: human life? God asks for very little as indicated by His planting only one forbidden tree among millions of trees. God's basic rules are these:

- Do not purposely injure others.
- Marriage is sacred, between one male and one female, husband and wife.
- Observe one day in respect for God, each week.
- Do not steal.
- Do not tell lies.
- Do not be unfaithful in marriage.
- Treat all others with respect, including God.

If we abide by these rules, the world would be a better place.

Judgment in the Garden

In the Garden of Eden stood three guilty beings about to learn their fate from the eternal judge. The first to be judged was the serpent.

Snakes were not able to speak at that time, neither are they able to speak today. It was Lucifer who gave the appearance that snakes were able to speak. Demons have the ability to speak, and they are able to affect both human and animal life. Because the snake was used to fool Eve, the serpent was first to be judged. The Lord said to the serpent, "Because you have done this, cursed are you above all livestock and above all beasts of the field; on your belly you shall go, and dust you shall eat all the days of your life" (Genesis 3:14).

Snakes were able to rotate their tail end in such a maneuver that as the body moved forward, the head was held high. God removed that ability from the serpent. Today, snakes are reduced to crawling on their belly with their head in the dust. Snakes remain among earth's most frightful creatures. Due to their secret or hidden movements, they pass with ease through tall grass and forests undetected and are among earth's most despised creatures.

Fallen Angels

The angel Lucifer was endowed with beauty and knowledge beyond all others. A number of angels admired Lucifer's beauty and brilliance and became intrigued by Lucifer. Such loftiness was more than Lucifer could graciously receive; he became vain. He thought, "I am as great as God. I will ascend above God's throne and rule the heavens and the earth." At the very moment of Christ's death on the cross, an enormous battle occurred, raging high in the heavens. This was not realized by people on earth. Scripture says:

> *Now war arose in heaven, Michael and his angels fighting against the dragon. And the dragon and his angels fought back, but he was defeated, and there was no longer any place for them in heaven. And the great dragon was thrown down, that ancient serpent, who is called the devil and Satan, the deceiver of the whole world—he was thrown down to the earth, and his angels were thrown down with him.*
>
> **—Revelation 12:7–9**

Doom of the Backslider

Angels were sinless; they are God's chosen and created holy beings. Angels lived in heaven with God, but those who fell with Lucifer were condemned to eternal hellfire due to their rebellion against God.

Second Peter 2:4 says, "God did not spare angels when they sinned, but cast them into hell." Peter ends the chapter with this summary of humanity:

> *For if, after they have escaped the defilements of the world through the knowledge of our Lord and Savior Jesus Christ, they are again entangled in them and overcome, the last state has become worse for them than the first. For it would have been better for them never to have known the way of righteousness than after knowing it to turn back from the holy commandment delivered to them. What the true proverb says has happened to them: "The dog returns to its own vomit, and the sow, after washing herself, returns to wallow in the mire."*
>
> **—2 Peter 2:20–22**

Who Will Enter Heaven?

The earth contains many religious people, but will they all go to heaven? One day as Jesus was passing through a village, someone asked Him, ""Lord, will those who are saved be few?" (Luke 13:23)? Jesus answered:

> *"Strive to enter through the narrow door. For many, I tell you, will seek to enter and will not be able. When once the master of the house has risen and shut the door, and you begin to stand outside and to knock at the door, saying, 'Lord, open to us,' then he will answer you, 'I do not know where you come from.' Then you will begin to say, 'We ate and drank in your presence, and you taught in our streets.' But he will say, 'I tell you, I do not know where you come from. Depart from me, all you workers of evil!' In that place there will be weeping and gnashing of teeth."*
>
> **—Luke 13:24–28**

On another occasion, Jesus offered a parable stating:

> *"The kingdom of heaven may be compared to a king who gave a wedding feast for his son. . . And those servants went out into the roads and gathered all whom they found, both bad and good. So the wedding hall was filled with guests. . . . "But when the king came in to look at the guests, he saw there a man who had no wedding garment. And he said to him, 'Friend, how did you get in here without a wedding garment?' And he was speechless. Then the king said to the attendants, 'Bind him hand and foot and cast him into the outer darkness. In that place there will be weeping and gnashing of teeth.' For many are called, but few are chosen."*
>
> **—Matthew 22:2, 10–14**

Temptation

In the wilderness, Jesus had fasted for forty days and was hungry. When a human is at their lowest point, temptation will be there to resolve the problem.

> *The devil showed Jesus all the kingdoms of the world and said, "To you I will give all this authority and their glory, for it has been delivered to me, and I give it to whom I will. If you, then, will worship me, it will all be yours."*
>
> **—Luke 4:6–7**

Jesus rejected Satan's invitation. The devil then led Jesus to the highest point of the temple and challenged Him to prove that He is God's son, by leaping from the pinnacle of the temple (Luke 4:9).

Suicide is a common temptation to those who become depressed due to circumstances beyond their control. Evil, depraved spirits (demons) speak to the individual, telling them that it would be very easy "to be rid of this problem; just jump"!

Satan, who knows more about the afterlife than we do, would not have tempted Christ had he believed there was no possibility of Christ's fall.

Judas, the Betrayer

Judas was one of the twelve disciples of Christ; he sold Jesus for thirty pieces of silver (Matthew 26:14–16).

With the silver, Judas suddenly became a wealthy man, and with that wealth, he bought a field where he could enjoy a peaceful existence. But when Judas learned of Jesus's death, he hanged himself (Matthew 27:1–10).

Apparently, the rope that Judas used was not adequate. The rope broke and caused Judas's body to plunge to the earth with such violence that his body burst open, spilling his intestines out on the field that Judas had purchased. People in Jerusalem heard about this, so they called that field, in their language, Akeldama, that is, "field of blood."

It was written in the book of Psalms, "May his days be few; may another take his office (Psalm 109:8)!

The Twelfth Disciple

After Judas's betrayal and death, it was decided that someone should fill the seat vacated by Judas. The eleven cast lots, and Matthias was chosen to be the twelfth disciple.

In regard to Judas, Jesus had said, "The Son of Man goes as it is written of him, but woe to that man by whom the Son of Man is betrayed! It would have been better for that man if he had not been born" (Matthew 26:24). Yes, Judas suffered a bad death, but the worst was yet to come! The book of Psalms contains historical notes on Jesus's betrayal by his friend. The psalmist wrote, "Even my close friend in whom I trusted, who ate my bread, has lifted his heel against me" (Psalm 41:9).

Life on earth, regardless of how majestic it is, cannot exceed 120 years (Genesis 6:31). Those who believe and accept God's salvation have everlasting life. Those who willfully reject or ignore God's gift would be better off if they had never existed. The author of Hebrews stated:

> *For it is impossible, in the case of those who have once been enlightened, who have tasted the heavenly gift, and have shared in the Holy Spirit, and have tasted the goodness of the word of God and the powers of the age to come, and then have fallen away, to restore them again to repentance, since they are crucifying once again the Son of God to their own harm and holding him up to contempt.*
>
> **—Hebrews 6:4–6**

Peter added his knowledge to the subject by stating:

> *For if, after they have escaped the defilements of the world through the knowledge of our Lord and Savior Jesus Christ, they are again entangled in them and overcome, the last state has become worse for*

them than the first. For it would have been better for them never to have known the way of righteousness than after knowing it to turn back from the holy commandment delivered to them. What the true proverb says has happened to them: "The dog returns to its own vomit, and the sow, after washing herself, returns to wallow in the mire."

—2 Peter 2:20–22

The Right Choice

Among humans, no one has demonstrated more desire to do God's will than Saul. Early in his life, Saul used his desire to please God by sending those who believed in Jesus to prison and death. When Jesus appeared to Saul on the road to Damascus, those who were with him saw nothing. In those few moments, Saul's life completely changed. The same intensity used to imprison people was instead used to verify that Jesus was truly God's sacrifice, who died for the sins of humanity. Those who receive Christ's death as their own substitute have everlasting life. If God granted Adam and Eve pardon via the sacrifice of a beast in Genesis 3, consider how much higher value would be in the death of a sinless human. Christ's death replaced animal sacrifice, not for just one year, but forever.

Animal sacrifice was a yearly chore. Christ's death was a one-time event that will remain forever. Because of Adam's sin, we all die. Because of Christ's death, we may choose to live forever! Jesus said, "And because lawlessness will be increased, the love of many will grow cold. But the one who endures to the end will be saved" (Matthew 24:12–13).

Chapter 7
Seed of the Woman

Due to the fact that the serpent was the creature first used by Satan to afflict humanity, the term serpent was adopted to also represent Lucifer, the devil. The snake is one of earth's most allusive creatures. Its reproductive seed quickly multiplies in secret, and its bite can lead to death. If Satan was to be compared to any creature, it would be the snake!

At the Fall, God made a prophetic statement four thousand years before the event occurred. God made a declaration of what would become of Satan at the appointed time: "I will put enmity between you and the woman, and between your offspring and her offspring" (Genesis 3:15).

From Adam's beginning, God revealed the plan of redemption, thousands of years in advance. A young virgin girl would conceive and give birth to the Prince of Peace (Isaiah 7:14; Matthew 1:23). The male child would belong to the lineage of Abraham and David and was to be called the "Son of God" (Matthew 1:1–17; Luke 1:26–35).

The child would be despised and rejected by his own people, beaten, and fastened to a cross with nails to hang until dead. One day this same Jesus will return to rule the nations with a rod of iron. This mighty warrior will one day rule over all earthly kingdoms. However, he first had to appear by the seed of a woman—not as a mighty warrior but as a helpless infant (Isaiah 53:1–12; Revelation 2:27).

Mary

Mary, a peasant girl, was engaged to Joseph for marriage, when Joseph discovered that she was pregnant. Joseph, in strict adherence to the Law, was overwhelmed with emotion; he immediately attempted to clear his good name from a scandal by sending Mary away.

If a man is engaged for marriage and his sweetheart is discovered to be pregnant and he knows that he is not the father, what then? Joseph was unprepared for such news; he thought, "How could I be such a fool. She acted so pure." Joseph, in grief and shame, was in the process of ending his promise of marriage by sending Mary away. Only an act of God could save this marriage. That is when an angel appeared to Joseph in a dream, saying that he was to marry Mary "for that which is conceived in her is from the Holy Spirit" (Matthew 1:20). The appearance of an angel from heaven would be a life-changing experience. Joseph became a new man after the angel's appearance. Joseph became a great husband to Mary and a great father to his children, though only a "stepfather" to Jesus.

Joseph taught Jesus the art of woodworking in which Jesus continued to the age of thirty. It is apparent, that if Mary was not a virgin at the time of Jesus's birth and if the Holy Spirit was not the cause of Jesus's birth, then Joseph lied, and Jesus was not the "Son of God." If that were true, we would have no sacrifice, and we would be lost in sin.

The Knowledge of God

The first sin was committed in the garden of Eden. To violate any one of God's commandments is sin. God could have killed Adam and Eve and then created new people. God knew that Adam and Eve would sin. God had a plan for each violation that occurred.

The Bible has numerous events that cause us to think that God was surprised at the outcome. Somehow, God knows each event with exact perception before it happens. How God knows each event of our tomorrows or even thousands of years in advance remains a mystery. We do know that what God said will occur; God's words are creative. As he speaks, the words take on meaningful appearance as unseen hands bring into existence the image of the spoken word.

Emmanuel

The prophets foretold that the virgin birth would occur in the town of Bethlehem. It would be followed by a pleading voice announcing the arrival of the Lord. The prophet John was that voice. Malachi foretold the coming of the Lord: "Prepare the way of the Lord." The child is Emmanuel and shall be called "Jesus" (Micah 5:2; Isaiah 40:3–5; Malachi 3:1; Matthew 1:21–23, 3:1–3).

Animal sacrifice was practiced from the days of Adam. Despite the death of an animal, the animal was not the equal of a human life. Man was made in God's image, not animals. It was God who declared, "The day you eat [of that tree] you shall surely die" (Genesis 2:17). Animals may disobey, but only humans can sin. It was God who spared human life by the substitution of an animal's death, but animals are not man's equal. Beasts provided a covering to hide Adam and Eve's shame before the eyes of God. In reality, their sin still existed. However, the sacrifice of an animal allowed humanity to exist until such a time when the true sacrifice would be made (Micah 5:2; Isaiah 40:3–5; Malachi 3:1; Matthew 1:21–23, 3:1–3).

The Holy One

No one on earth is guilt-free. All have become contaminated by sin. We all are Adam's descendants, regardless of our differences. To be free of sin, someone would have to appear from a different world that was sin-free. Throughout the Old Testament, we have hints, suggestions, and facts that, in actuality, a being would come from heaven having no sin. The seed of life came from God, not a sinful man. Jesus was known as "The Son of God," uncontaminated by sin.

The author of Hebrews wrote that "It is impossible for the blood of bulls and goats to take away sins" (Hebrews 10:4; cf. Psalm 40:6–8). Then he referred to the true sacrifice of Christ, "A body you prepared for me" (Hebrews 10:5). These words describe the purpose of Christ's advent. His home is heaven, yet He resided on earth, in order that mankind may have the choice to live or die.

Show Me God

In the beginning, God created the heavens and the earth. The Genesis record also states, "Let us make man in our image, after our likeness" (Genesis 1:26).

Who is "us" as stated in creation story? The reference to "us" clarifies the meaning of the term God, not as a single Being, rather as a plurality of Beings. John stated that God was seven spirits who formed one God (Revelation 3:1). If man was created in God's image as stated, could the human body have a resemblance to the Godhead? The human body consists of two essential elements: a head and body.

Remove one of those two, and there would be nothing. The head has the ability to think yet performs no physical act. All the movements of the body are a result of thoughts located in the head. The arm and the leg each has a unique qualification for particular movements as directed by

the head. It was Phillip, a disciple of Christ, who interrupted Jesus as he was teaching the people in regard to God: Philip said, "Lord, show us the Father, and it is enough for us" (John 14:8). Jesus answered:

> *"Have I been with you so long, and you still do not know me, Philip? Whoever has seen me has seen the Father. How can you say, 'Show us the Father'? Do you not believe that I am in the Father and the Father is in me? The words that I say to you I do not speak on my own authority, but the Father who dwells in me does his works. Believe me that I am in the Father and the Father is in me, or else believe on account of the works themselves."*
>
> **—John 14 :9–11**

No mortal being could cause actual miracles to occur. If God created heaven and earth and all that exists, He easily has the power to perform as He pleases (Romans 1:18–25).

God who is invisible to all can only be seen if He appears in a visible form. The air we breathe is invisible, yet we are able to detect air by its movements. We believe in God because of His works. No man can see God and live, yet each day we recognize His creation and realize that God is real (Exodus 33:20). God has the ability to appear at the same moment in as many forms and locations as He pleases. God is in Hell, yet the fire is unaware of His presence (Psalm 139:7–12).

God is on the bottom of the sea; He knows each star by name and even knows when a sparrow falls to the earth (Psalm 147:4; Matthew 10:29–31). God knows the number of hairs on each head and is emotionally involved with His creation (Luke 12:7; 2 Peter 3:9).

God, who had no beginning, likely created objects and universes beyond human ability to number. He existed billions of trillions of years in the remote past, and we are unable to grasp a being who exists without a beginning. Because God always existed, we also exist. Evolution has no explanation that is worthy of respect as to how all this stuff came into existence. Jesus, the miracle worker, God the Father, still exist in the lives of many people, who witness His goodness each day.

Who Is Jesus?

The Genesis record states, "Let us make man in our image, after our likeness" (Genesis 1:26).

Is there a Godhead, a plurality of beings that form a single entity known as God? They are revealed in the New Testament as the Father, Son, and Holy Spirit." One member of the Godhead came to the earth in the flesh of a human. A virgin girl gave birth to a male infant, who was named Jesus. As Jesus became a young man, He worked as a carpenter alongside His stepfather. His real identity was not realized until it became evident that there was no obstacle that Jesus could not correct, with a single spoken word. Miracles instantly came into existence. Water became wine. Jesus spoke to a storm that was about to sink their boat. With a single command, violent winds ceased, and the raging sea instantly became calm. Even the disciples became terrified saying, "Who then is this, that even the wind and the sea obey him" (Mark 4:41)?

Jesus fed over five thousand people with a boy's lunch that the lad had in a basket. After all the people had eaten until they could eat no more, twelve baskets of leftovers were gathered (John 6:5–14). A similar miracle occurred that involved four thousand people. The massive crowds that followed Christ struggled with each other to get close enough to hear Jesus's words and witness the miracles that He performed. For three days the people had followed, and Jesus had compassion on them because they had nothing to eat. A little fish, a little bread—enough for Jesus and His disciples—was all they had. Jesus told His disciples to have the people sit down. Giving thanks over the food, Jesus broke the bread and the fish, telling His disciples to pass the food. As they passed the bread and the fish, the food continued to multiply. When the people wanted no more, the disciples picked up seven baskets full of broken pieces that were left over (Mark 8:1–9).

Jesus touched the sick and they instantly became well. Jesus spoke to the leper and the blind, and instantly they were cured. Jesus displayed authority over all elements that no human was able to perform naturally. Jesus displayed power that only God has. Yes, Jesus was clothed in human flesh, but yet He was God.

Chapter 8

The Arrest of Jesus

While thousands followed Jesus daily, His fame became renowned. Others became hostile toward this Jesus whom they have never met. The religious authorities of the day could not tolerate this new person who was invading their official domain.

This newcomer was not educated as a priest, and He was from a questionable background. He was asserting authority on His own without consent of the high priests. This Jesus was not a part of the established order and was regarded as a radical. That was the thinking of the religious leaders. No one despised this Jesus or His followers more than a man named Saul.

There was an official demand for the arrest and investigation of a man named Jesus. He was arrested by the priests and then taken to the High Priest. The questioning of Jesus proved nothing. They interrogated Him: "Did you not say?" or "Were those not your words?" Unable to legally carry out the death penalty, the Jewish leaders brought Jesus to the Roman governor, Pilate.

Pilate became unwilling to have Jesus put to death after realizing that the Jews' accusations against Jesus were illogical, none of which was deserving of death. Pilate, desiring to dispense of the matter, sent Jesus to be tried by the King Herod.

King Herod was very glad to see Jesus because of Christ's fame. Herod hoped to see Jesus perform a miracle or two. Upon Jesus's arrival, Herod questioned Him at length, but Jesus answered the King nothing. Herod became very angry and, in a rage, had his soldiers dress Jesus as a King and sent Him back to Pilate. This caused a friendship to bloom between the two rulers (Luke 23:8–12).

The Israelites had been told some seven hundred years before, that Christ was to visit earth. It was Isaiah who said, "The Lord himself will give you a sign. Behold, the virgin shall conceive and bear a son, and shall call his name Immanuel" (Isaiah 7:14). The name Immanuel, simply means, "God is with us." The declaration of a virgin birth carries the scorn of the ungodly, but the righteous will inherit everlasting life.

God's Many Faces

God, who is invisible, conversed with Adam in the garden. It is not likely that Adam had a conversation with a voice in the sky. God likely appeared as a mortal man who spoke. Both Adam and Eve heard the sound of God walking in the garden. Spirits do not cause sound as they move!

Both Cain and Abel had conversations with God in a rather relaxed manner (Genesis 4:3–7). Noah conversed with God on numerous occasions regarding the construction of the ark (Genesis 6:7, 13–21).

Abram, who became Abraham, had numerous conversations with God, not in prayer but person to person. In Jehovah's first appearance to Abram, God introduced himself by stating, "I am God Almighty; walk before me, and be blameless" (Genesis 17:1).

Later, God again visited Abraham. As the day progressed, Abraham invited God and His friends to stay for dinner. God and His friends, along with Abraham, had what could be considered as earth's first gourmet meal (Genesis 18:1–8).

Throughout the Old Testament, God made Himself known through revelation, visions, dreams, and appearances. God spoke to Hagar, informing her that she was pregnant with a son and that she was to name him Ishmael (Genesis 16:13–15).

Jacob wrestled with God all night. As a result, Jacob's hip became dislocated. The rest of Jacob's life, he walked with a limp. No one wrestles with God all night without being changed. To Jacob, God said, "Your name shall no longer be called Jacob, but Israel, for you have striven with God and with men" (Genesis 32:28).

The Ancestry of Mary and Joseph

Immanuel translated implies, "God with us." Matthew's genealogy of Abraham's descendants appears to be in order. Abraham to Joseph was forty-two generations at which time Jesus was born. Joseph claimed that he was not the father, neither was any other man involved. Both Joseph and Mary were descendants of Abraham as was David (Matthew 1:6).

The seed of the woman was literally fulfilled by the life and death of Jesus. As God stated in the garden of Eden so long ago the seed of the woman (Jesus Christ) would bruise the head of the serpent (Lucifer). The head contains the authority for good or evil.

During the scuffle that took place on the cross, the serpent bruised the heel of Jesus, who appeared from the seed of the woman. Nails were driven through Jesus's hands and feet. However, Satan's authority over the lives of people was forever diminished, and he awaits a sorrowful existence, destined for an eternal world of fire. Christ's death on the cross ended Lucifer's authority over the earth. Satan will continue to cause illness as he did with Job and tempt people to do wrong, yet his freedom of days is numbered, so that he, in a panic, attempts to cause sorrow and mischief. In a rage, Lucifer is aware that his days are numbered. Lucifer and his comrades will be confined in Hell; then he will trouble the world no more (1 Peter 5:8; Revelation 20:10).

The Scourging of Christ

Pilate's difficulty was that he could find no fault in Jesus, yet he desired to please the religious authorities. The religious leaders requested that the Roman military execute Jesus, so the synagogue could continue with God's work as they understood it to be.

The opposition to Christ is what caused God's plan to come into existence. By attempting to appease the religious leaders, Pilate unknowingly fulfilled the Scripture. Pilate, not willing to have Christ killed, thought that having Jesus scourged would satisfy their demands, but Pilate was wrong. The prophetic utterance given by the Prophet Isaiah, described the unhuman scourging given to Christ, prior to his crucifixion: "I gave my back to those who strike, and my cheeks to those who pull out the beard; I hid not my face from disgrace and spitting" (Isaiah 50:6).

Jewish law limited whippings to a maximum of forty lashes (Deuteronomy 25:3). However, Jesus was not punished in accordance with Jewish law. Jesus was given to the Roman authorities who had mastered cruelty. Those Romans chosen to scourge the guilty appeared to be men who enjoyed their work; they not only scourged Jesus, but they took pleasure in torture and seeing others suffer.

The guilty was stripped of all clothing. Naked they were bent over, their hands tied to a post approximately two feet in height. Stooped over, all his manhood was exposed to the one holding the whip. Those who survived the beating would never be the same again. Jesus was whipped to the point that his bones became visible. What would His face look like after the tormentors pulled His beard out from the flesh in which His hair had grown? Soldiers had to hold Jesus while others pulled. One man alone could not pull out His beard; it required a group of tormentors.

One of the soldiers cut branches from a thorn bush, twisting them together to form a crown. He then placed the crown on Jesus's head. The soldiers continued to have a good time, dancing around Jesus, declaring, "Hail, King of the Jews" (Mark 15:18)! They struck Jesus on the thorny crown with the flat side of their swords, causing the thorns to penetrate the scalp as the blood flowed down the face of the One who had created the universe. They spit on Jesus's face as they danced, revealing their contempt for the God who created them.

The Handsome Lucifer

It was an angel named Lucifer who attempted to silence Christ desiring that Jesus would not die on the cross as required by God. Lucifer desired to replace God by becoming the only god of this world.

It was Lucifer, who in the past, said to Jesus, after He had fasted forty days without food, "All these [kingdoms] I will give you, if you will fall down and worship me" (Mark 4:9). Lucifer would not have tempted Christ had he believed that Jesus could not be tempted. Lucifer relentlessly tempts each person to do wrong.

The death of Jesus on the cross would end Lucifer's authority on earth. No mortal human could have survived the beatings Christ endured and still be alive. But He who walked on the water, He who the winds obeyed was more than mortal man. It was because of His stripes of physical pain that we can be made whole: "But he was pierced for our transgressions; he was crushed for our iniquities; upon him was the chastisement that brought us peace, and with his wounds we are healed" (Isaiah 53:9).

Chapter 9

The Passover Lamb

The body of Jesus was in such a bloody and shocking appearance that there are no words to describe how He looked. Despite Jesus's appearance, they had to hand Him over to Pilate to determine His guilt or innocence, in the presence of a massive audience.

All this took place at the Passover, which was and continues to be celebrated each spring. It was to be a lasting ordinance from their captivity from Egypt. The festival would continue for several days. Passover was the special event of the year: people gathered from far and near (Exodus 12:14).

Strong substances must have been used to stop Jesus's bleeding. When Jesus was sufficiently clean, they dressed him in a long robe and then sent Him out to meet Pilate, who stood before a large number of people.

It was the custom on Passover to release one prisoner from captivity as a memorial to the Jews' release from Egyptian bondage. Pilate selected a notorious criminal named Barabbas. Not only was Barabbas a thief, but he was also a murderer (Luke 23:19).

Jesus and Barabbas stood side by side. Pilate at length gave a review of the crimes and murder committed by this Barabbas. On the other side, was a well-known man who had fed the hungry and helped those who were sick. His name was Jesus. "But they all cried out together, 'Away with this man, and release to us Barabbas'" (Luke 23:18). Pilate pleaded, "Why? What evil has he done" (Luke 23:22)?

But the people insisted that Barabbas be released and that Jesus should die. The crowd became loud and roared constantly. Pilate again stated that he could find no fault in Jesus and that even King Herod, after examining Jesus, could find no fault in him. "But they were urgent, demanding with loud cries that he should be crucified. And their voices prevailed. So Pilate decided that their demand should be granted" (Luke 23:23–24).

Three times Pilate attempted to release Jesus, but that was not to be. The people demanded that Jesus be crucified and that Barabbas be set free.

The Cross

Pilate submitted to the decision of the people, and Jesus was taken into custody. The guilty one must walk to his crucifixion. Jesus was required to carry the crossbar on which his hands would be nailed. The crossbar may have weighed forty to sixty pounds.

The "cross" is so named because the crossbar crosses the pole to which it is attached. The pole was a permanent structure used repeatedly. The pole, would be similar to a telephone pole in that it was set at least four feet into the earth to keep it upright.

The Roman soldiers nailed Jesus to the cross. Psalm 22:16 says, "They have pierced my hands and feet."

Jesus's fame rivaled that of the governor, possibly even the Emperor, and the men who crucified Jesus, desired a trophy for crucifying one having such fame. The only object of value that belonged to Jesus was his clothing. So the soldiers divided His clothing among them. One garment was seamless, woven in one piece from top to bottom. For that garment, they cast lots (John 19:23–24). Over a thousand years earlier, the psalmist had written: "They divide my garments among them, and for my clothing they cast lots" (Psalm 22:18).

Naked, Jesus hung on the cross. Again, the psalmist recorded the exact thoughts of Christ as he hung there visible to all who passed by: "They stare and gloat over me" (Psalm 22:17).

On the Roman crosses hung three men. Two were criminals; Jesus hung between the two:

> *One of the criminals who were hanged railed at him, saying, "Are you not the Christ? Save yourself and us!" But the other rebuked him, saying, "Do you not fear God, since you are under the same sentence of condemnation? And we indeed justly, for we are receiving the due reward of our deeds; but this man has done nothing wrong." And he said, "Jesus, remember me when you come into your kingdom." And he said to him, "Truly, I say to you, today you will be with me in paradise."*
>
> **—Luke 23:39–43**

The mystery of salvation becomes clear when we recognize that we do not inherit everlasting life by our efforts or works. It was Jesus who paid our ticket to journey from earth to that land in the sky. Regardless of our good works, we remain sinful. Like Adam, we became sinful and unable to change; we are condemned because of sin. The death of an animal kept man out of hell, but not sufficiently clean for heaven. To become pure enough for heaven requires perfection. Jesus was perfect, and He died in our place. Sin came into the world because of one man, Adam. By one perfect man who died in our place, we are allowed to receive Christ's perfection as our own. We will die because of Adam's sin, but like Christ, we will rise from our dead bodies with bodies that will live forever. Like the thief, if we admit our guilt, turn from our wicked ways, and ask Christ to enter our lives, then we will be ready for heaven (Romans 2:3, 4:5–6).

The psalmist describes Jesus's thirst on the cross: "My strength is dried up like a potsherd, and my tongue sticks to my jaws" (Psalm 22:15). Suffering on the cross, Jesus uttered the words, "I thirst" (John 19:28). A soldier quickly soaked a sponge in vinegar and lifted it up for Jesus to drink. Jesus took a sip, bowed his head, and gave up His spirit (John 19:30). Long before the crucifixion, David wrote: "For my thirst they gave me sour wine to drink" (Psalm 69:21).

The following day was the Sabbath—not a normal Sabbath, for this was the last Sabbath of the Passover, which was the most honored and celebrated event of the year. This Sabbath would be the climax of the celebration, and for this special Sabbath, Jewish law forbid that bodies be left on the crosses.

The religious leaders begged Pilate, who had the authority, to have the bodies removed for this special day. Before the bodies could be removed from the crosses, someone had to verify that each person was dead. To hasten the process, the prisoners' legs were broken the day before.

The soldiers broke the legs of the two criminals. When they came to Jesus, he was already dead. One of the soldiers pierced Jesus's side with a spear; blood and water ran out. The Prophet had said: "He keeps all his bones, not one of them is broken" (Psalm 34:20; cf. Numbers 9:12).

Zechariah wrote: "When they look on me, on him whom they have pierced, they shall mourn for him, as one mourns for an only child, and weep bitterly over him, as one weeps over a firstborn" (Zechariah 12:10). David wrote: "A company of evildoers encircles me; they have pierced my hands and feet—I can count all my bones—they stare and gloat over me; they divide my garments among them, and for my clothing they cast lots" (Psalm 22:16–18).

Darkness covered the land. The earth shook with such violence that rocks literally split open. Tombs that were sealed opened. Holy people who had died were seen walking the streets. The soldiers who were on guard became terrified exclaiming, "Truly this was the Son of God" (Matthew 27:54).

Chapter 10

Earth's First Tabernacle

Several centuries passed from the day God delivered Abraham's children out of slavery. Moses became the voice of God to the people. The Ark of the Covenant became the most sacred object in ancient Judaism, constructed under God's direction to Moses. Israel needed a house in which to place the Ark. The house was to be for temporary use, not permanent. Initially, the entire structure was a tent, divided into two rooms. The first room was called the Holy Place; it was restricted to priests only even though it was less formal than the second room. The second room, Most Holy Place, was the most sacred location on earth. No one could go into or even look into the Most Holy Place where God resided. No human was holy after Adam's sin. This was God's room; sinners may not enter, for all are sinful.

Uzzah, who was not a priest though a good man, reached out to steady the Ark as the priests were transporting it. That irreverent act cost Uzzah his life; he died beside the Ark of God (1 Samuel 6:6–7). No unauthorized person was to touch what God had made holy.

Though he was sinful, the High Priest was permitted to prepare himself for entry into God's room on behalf of the people—but only on one designated day each year. The Tabernacle was located in a fenced yard that had an entry gate, a bronze altar, and a bronze basin. The priest would first cleanse himself using water from the basin (Exodus 30:17–21).

Second, the priest must sacrifice a bull for his own sins; then on the bronze altar the priest would sacrifice a ram for the people. Then the High Priest will take the ram's blood with him when he entered God's room (Exodus 29:10).

To seal God's room from all others, a substantial rug-like curtain divided the inner room from the larger room. In God's room was the Ark of the Covenant, a container roughly thirty inches high by eighteen inches wide. The entire chest was made of wood covered with pure gold. The Ark contained the two stone tablets on which God had written the Ten Commandments with His own finger, a pot of manna as a reminder of what had happened in the past, and Aaron's rod that budded (Numbers 17:10–11; Deuteronomy 10:1–2). In my opinion, the Ark probably exists somewhere today, securely held by scholars of Judaism.

The tent structure (tabernacle) was God's temporary dwelling place until such a time when He would no longer abide in a structure made by human hands. It took seven years for Solomon to build a sumptuous temple. The temple in Jesus's day had even more grandeur; this second temple required forty-six years to complete (John 2:20). After Christ's death, God moved into the lives of His people who became His living church, replacing the cold structure of a temple. Even so, humanity was intent on building "God's house."

In 70 AD, the Roman military came into Jerusalem and completely destroyed the city. The temple, which had been constructed to last many generations, was demolished such that no two stones remained together. Many people ran; some fought; those who survived entered other countries, but not all were greeted with cheer.

Two thousand years passed after the devastation of Israel. Many surviving Israelites had escaped empty-handed. In despair, they endeavored to exist. Today Israel is back in the neighborhood surrounded by intolerant neighbors who fail to understand kindness. One day the Christ, whom they crucified, will return and establish a kingdom that will last thousands of years.

Demise of the Tabernacle

The moment Jesus died on the cross, the heavy curtain that separated God's room from the world tore open from top to bottom, exposing God's room to the world. God's room had become void of God. Jesus's sacrificial death replaced the constant need for animal sacrifice, which covered and concealed sin. Jesus's death removed the stain of sin forever. Humanity—rich or poor, priest or peasant—all may approach God, speaking to Him as if they were face to face.

The Torn Curtain

The curtain in the temple tore apart. The torn curtain ended animal sacrifice, which began in the Garden of Eden. Sturdy constructed temples still exist, but without sacrifices. No animal has been sacrificed for over two thousand years. What has become of all those who have died without a sacrifice? Jesus was the Father's sacrifice given for all who receive God's gift. Jesus is without sin—God's perfect and only sacrifice who can enter heaven directly.

The Mystery of Salvation

Animal sacrifice in the garden of Eden provided a covering for Adam and Eve's naked bodies. It hid their sin but failed to remove the sin. As a result, their sin kept them out of heaven and placed them in a holding place, on or near the earth. Jesus called that place Abraham's bosom (Luke 16:19–31).

Only those who have completed cleansing from their sins may enter heaven. Only the death of Jesus on our behalf makes this possible. All those who were willing to obey the law given Moses by God were unable to enter heaven because their sins were covered by the animal sacrifice, but not removed.

Adam was created as a perfect human. It required a perfect likeness to die on Adam's behalf. Such a being did not exist on earth. A perfect human had to come from heaven, perfect in every respect, uncontaminated by any of earth's many sins. That perfect one was Jesus. We are not perfect and are unable to enter heaven. Those who regret their sin and ask God for forgiveness receive God's gift of everlasting life. Jesus took my place in death that I may live forever. Two criminals were crucified at the same time as Jesus; one was abusive in death, but the other asked for mercy saying, "Jesus, remember me when you come into your kingdom." And he said to him, "Truly, I say to you, today you will be with me in paradise" (Luke 23:42–43).

Chapter 11

Saul's Fame

Saul's fame began as a result of his anger toward the new religion, which became known as Christianity. The Law given by God to Moses was not to be questioned rather obeyed.

Stephen

An Old Testament scholar named, Stephen, embraced Christ's new message of repentance that was contradictory to the rituals that have been practiced for many centuries. Both the people and the temple were pleased with the existing arrangement and not prepared for any drastic changes.

Had Stephen embraced the new doctrine and kept it to himself that would have been acceptable. But on a street corner, stood Stephen, announcing in a loud voice that the day of Moses had passed. Today was a new day in which Christ's death provided what animal sacrifice could not provide; Stephen's message was true. But people could not believe in such a drastic change to their lifestyle, and Saul was there also.

Stephen had attracted large numbers of annoyed people who began shouting insults at him as he spoke. They became so angry that many desired to shut Stephen's mouth, which they did by the Law of Moses. Stoning was an appropriate death for those who spoke against Moses and the Law. It was this event that began Saul's crusade to end Christianity (Acts 7:58, 8:1).

Saul, in full agreement with Stephen's death, began a crusade against the Christian church in Jerusalem. Saul began ravaging those known to be Christ's followers. Entering house after house, Saul with a group of men, dragged off men and women, placing them in prison (Acts 8:1–3).

Then Saul met the risen Christ, and Saul became a new man.

The New Saul

Within several days of Saul's conversion, Saul spent his days in Damascus with disciples who had lived with Christ. There he learned details not available in print. Devoted as Saul was to Judaism, his devotion to the new cause for Christ was just as intense as it had been in his former life—in his opposition against Christianity.

Immediately after Saul's departure from the disciples, Saul began to proclaim Jesus in the synagogues, declaring that Jesus was the Son of God. All those who heard him were amazed saying, "Is not this the man who made havoc in Jerusalem of those who called upon this name" (Acts 9:21)? But Saul kept increasing in strength and confounding the Jews who lived at Damascus by proving that this Jesus is the Christ.

Several days elapsed before people plotted to kill Saul. Saul became aware that men were watching the gates night and day to seize him. In the dark of night, Saul's friends smuggled him to safety putting him in a large basket. When Saul attempted to associate with other Christians, who were unfamiliar with Saul's conversation, they were afraid, not believing that he had changed (Acts 9).

At his conversion, Saul was smitten by God so that he instantly became blind. Then a man by the name of Ananias was told by God, that he was to lay his hands on blind Saul so that Saul could regain his sight. But Ananias was afraid to do so. The Lord said to Ananias, "He [Saul] is a chosen instrument of mine to carry my name before the Gentiles and kings and the children of Israel. For I will show him how much he must suffer for the sake of my name" (Acts 9:15–16). No human, apart from Jesus, endured more suffering by the hands of men than Saul.

If there was one person or a gathering of many, Saul would dominate the conversation by preaching Christ. Saul spoke with such passion that people believed his words or became visibly angry. Numerous times Saul was beaten or mistreated, and even the high priests who once loved him, no longer welcomed Saul.

Lystra was a Roman province consisting of both Jews and Gentiles. The life and death of Jesus was the cause of major devastation to the nation of Israel. Its people were scattered throughout many nations, unable to return to their land. Even the great temple that required years to construct, in a single day would be turned into rumble.

Two thousand years of wandering and death have passed, and now the people are trickling back into the promised land, but all is not peace.

Chapter 12

The Cost of Salvation

While Peter was with other disciples involved with matters in their homeland, Saul, Barnabas, and John preached Christ to the Gentile world. There is nothing to suggest that Peter ever traveled beyond Jerusalem. Saul, the dominant speaker, so angered some of the Jews, that they invoked the Mosaic Law in regard to capital punishment. The Law demanded death by stoning for those who deliberately were disobedient to the Law. Saul's words were blasphemous against Moses and Judaism, insisted his opponents. Saul was forcefully removed to a favorable location where he had been sentenced to die by stoning, and that should be the end of the story.

The practice of stoning required several young men who were able to throw rocks with accuracy and force. One rock thrown violently to the head could cause the person to become unconscious or even die. Facial and body fractures as well as broken bones would be expected. When the victim no longer had breath, he was pronounced dead.

Saul was stoned. Examining his body, they were convinced that Saul was dead. They then dragged his limp body to the town dump outside the city, where they disposed of the body. After the mob had departed, a group of believers gathered around Saul's "dead" body, earnestly asking God to restore life to Saul. That same day, Saul's eyes opened, and he stood to his feet and returned to the same city that stoned him. As Saul preached the Gospel, people realized the miracle that they had witnessed, and many became disciples (Acts 14:19–22).

Saul's Visit to Paradise

Fourteen years had passed after the day of Saul's stoning. For the first time in Saul's many writings, he revealed a little of his journey in the afterlife. Saul was caught up into the third heaven, which is called paradise. There Saul saw and heard words that he was forbidden to reveal (2 Corinthians 12:2–4).

Saul then revealed why he was beaten, robbed, and imprisoned, more than other disciples. Why? Saul states that he had been given an abundance of revelations. In God's mercy, so that Saul would not become vain, Satan became a messenger used by God to buffet Saul lest he became exalted above measure. Saul asked God three times to remove his abnormal amount of suffering. God said, no: "My grace is sufficient for you, for my power is made perfect in weakness" (2 Corinthians 12:9). Through pain, Saul was able to trust in God, unlike Satan, who became vain, due to his success and brilliance.

The Missionary

Saul traveled through a number of villages, cities, and nations that were Gentile. Saul proclaimed a strange new message to a pagan world that was filled with elicit witchcraft and strange gods. Saul's message was unique in that he proclaimed that there was only one true God, who had no beginning, had always existed, and is the creator of all that exists.

Saul explained that he was one of God's messengers to communicate God's message to those who will hear and obey God's Word. Saul proved that he was God's messenger by placing his hands on the sick, asking God to heal them, and they were instantly healed. This convinced many that Saul's message was real, and they, too, became disciples; yet others regarded the miracles with scorn, stating that the illusions of magic and other supposed supernatural effects were a pretense, not real. Jesus taught:

> *Enter by the narrow gate. For the gate is wide and the way is easy that leads to destruction, and those who enter by it are many. For the gate is narrow and the way is hard that leads to life, and those who find it are few.*
>
> **—Matthew 7:13–14**

The Council

A number of Christian Jews from far and wide began gathering at a location in Jerusalem. Saul and Barnabas also came. Saul had given a glowing report of what was achieved among the Gentiles, when a number of the delegates objected stating: "It is necessary to circumcise them and to order them to keep the law of Moses" (Acts 15:5).

This refusal to accept Gentiles as truly converted caused an uproar among the delegation. The Apostles came together to look into this matter, and after much debate, it was decided that the uncircumcised were saved through the grace of God. While people can pretend conversion, these Gentiles also had received the Holy Spirit—the same as those in the Upper Room, and that cannot be pretended (Acts 15:1–12).

Saul later explained that the formal, yet sincere religion from Saul's past, was dedicated to God; yet Saul had been wrong in so many ways. But when Saul met Jesus, face to face, Saul's life was forever changed. The Holy Spirit came into his life, and Saul experienced a power beyond his expectation. Saul prayed for the sick, and they were healed. He cast out evil spirits from people and spoke with a power that changed lives. Saul credited his new power to the day Ananias placed his hands on him. Saul was not only converted but also was filled with the Holy Spirit (Acts 9:17).

Chapter 13
The Holy Spirit

The salvation of Jesus's Apostles was not in question. The disciples were as ready for heaven as any human could be. Jesus died and shed His blood for their redemption. Because Jesus lives, the redeemed will rise from their dead bodies and live forever in that new world.

Yet, there is more in store for God's redeemed people. Jesus's disciples were in need of a new source of power. In the Old Testament, there were the prophets. In the New Testament, Jesus gave his disciples power even to heal the sick and cast out unclean spirits (Matthew 10:1).

Then Jesus sent out seventy more to go to every city with the message. The seventy returned with joy saying, "Lord, even the demons are subject to us in your name" (Luke 10:17)!

During the years that Jesus was on earth, God's messengers had a power that exceeded human ability. A new source of power was needed to demonstrate that God still existed after Jesus's ascension. Before his ascension, Jesus said to his disciples, "And these signs will accompany those who believe: in my name they will cast out demons; they will speak in new tongues; . . . they will lay their hands on the sick, and they will recover" (Mark 16:17–18).

Even though they pray for the sick, all are not healed; yet many are. In a perfect world, there would be no sickness. Supernatural power was given to those who believe. Those who failed to believe obviously had no spiritual power: just talk.

Jesus said, "And behold, I am sending the promise of my Father upon you. But stay in the city until you are clothed with power from on high"(Luke 24:49). In John's Gospel, Jesus said, "As the Father has sent me, even so I am sending you" (John 20:21). In Acts, Jesus was quoted as saying, "John baptized with water, but you will be baptized with the Holy Spirit not many days from now " (John 1:5). Then Jesus added, "You will receive power when the Holy Spirit has come upon you" (John 1:8).

> *When the day of Pentecost arrived, they were all together in one place. And suddenly there came from heaven a sound like a mighty rushing wind, and it filled the entire house where they were sitting. And divided tongues as of fire appeared to them and rested on each one of them. And they were all filled with the Holy Spirit and began to speak in other tongues as the Spirit gave them utterance.*
>
> **—Acts 2:1–4**

This forceful display of the Holy Spirit's entry to earth was extremely obvious. In the garden of Eden, God conversed with man. In the New Testament, God became human. With the disappearance of Jesus, came the Holy Spirit who will remain in power until Jesus returns to earth.

The "other tongues" would indicate that they spoke languages not their native tongue. A group of one hundred twenty people were all speaking in languages that were foreign to each of them. There was such excitement and loud, joyful praise that they never before experienced before.

The Holy Spirit versus Salvation

Pentecost was not the story of salvation. Each person who received the Holy Spirit was a chosen child of God, paid for by Christ's death. Pentecost is the unequaled, distinct story of how God's people are to have spiritual power in their lives after their conversion.

A disciple named Philip, proclaimed Christ to gatherings of people in Samaria. His sermons were accompanied by prayer for the sick in which paralytics and cripples were healed. There was great excitement in the city because of Philip's good news about God's Kingdom, and many were baptized in water—both men and women.

In Acts we read:

> *Now when the apostles at Jerusalem heard that Samaria had received the word of God, they sent to them Peter and John, who came down and prayed for them that they might receive the Holy Spirit, for he had not yet fallen on any of them, but they had only been baptized in the name of the Lord Jesus. Then they laid their hands on them and they received the Holy Spirit.*
>
> **—Acts 8:14–17**

When Simon saw that the Spirit was given at the laying on of the Apostle's hands, he offered them money and said, "Give me this power also, so that anyone on whom I lay my hands may receive the Holy Spirit" (Acts 8:19). The Holy Spirit was given in addition to the gift of salvation. Jesus died for our sins, so that we may have everlasting life. The gift of the Holy Spirit was given after the gift of salvation had become provided. The gift of salvation and the receiving of the Holy Spirit were two distinct subjects and gifts. Salvation provides eternal life. The gift of the Holy Spirit provides a power that exceeds human capability.

The late Kathryn Kuhlman, an ordained Baptist minister of the nineteenth century, was such a person that she filled large auditoriums.

Wherever she went, thousands of people gathered to hear her words and witness the many miracles that occurred at each gathering. For several years, she ministered at Carnegie Auditorium in Pittsburgh, Pennsylvania. There have been numerous others who through their prayers, were healed of aliments as people were in biblical times. It was Jesus who said, "And these signs will accompany those who believe: in my name they will cast out demons; they will speak in new tongues; . . . they will lay their hands on the sick, and they will recover" (Mark 16:17–18). Was Jesus just a compulsive person to lie, or was he God? Saul wrote, "Do your best to present yourself to God as one approved, a worker who has no need to be ashamed, rightly handling the word of truth" (2 Timothy 2:15).

The Holy Spirit was not to provide salvation, but to provide power to those who believed. "And they were all filled with the Holy Spirit and began to speak in other tongues as the Spirit gave them utterance" (Acts 2:4).

People, from many nations, who had gathered in Jerusalem for Pentecost, were speaking different languages, not just mumbling words. The hundred twenty people were so loud in their ecstasy that other people began to gather, wondering what caused the ruckus. People were speaking in languages unfamiliar in Jerusalem. Yet people from other nations were able to hear their own tongue being uttered by people who had no knowledge of speaking their language. People were instantly speaking languages unknown to them, clearly and without an accent.

Saul's Explanation

Saul who had been persecuting the believers at the time of Pentecost, after his conversion, went on to explain the Holy Spirit. There are gifts assigned with the receiving of the Holy Spirit. Saul, the intellectual, who by his own understanding had attempted to end Christianity, had a complete change of heart. Saul became the main spokesperson for Christianity. Saul was the only person to logically describe the correct reasoning and doctrine of the Holy Spirit.

Saul defined the gift of tongues given by the Holy Spirit:

> *For one who speaks in a tongue speaks not to men but to God; for no one understands him, but he utters mysteries in the Spirit. . . . The one who speaks in a tongue builds up himself, but the one who prophesies builds up the church.*
>
> **—1 Corinthians 14:2, 4**

On the day of Pentecost, people came to the Holy Land in honor of their mysterious departure from slavery. It was a celebration unequal to any other event. Jewish people who lived in many nations and spoke the language of their adopted nations came to Jerusalem for this special event. God would also use that day to highlight the arrival of the Holy Spirit.

A New Language

The adoption of a new language is extremely difficult. Man can journey to the moon in relevantly a short time, learning a new language requires many years. On the day of Pentecost, people spoke languages unknown to them with perfection—a human function that is not humanly possible. Those who receive the Holy Spirit have a gift to speak the language of the Holy Spirit. Many have the Holy Spirit without releasing their tongues; it is a gift given for their edification. Salvation is a gift accepted by very few. Some real Christians fail to understand the mystery of tongues and its value. The gift of tongues is voluntary to speak, not a forced language. The gift is a gift, not a required language.

Saul stated, "For one who speaks in a tongue speaks not to men but to God; for no one understands him, but he utters mysteries in the Spirit"

(1 Corinthians 14:2). Then Saul goes on to say, "I thank God that I speak in tongues more than all of you" (1 Corinthians 14:18).

Not all believers speak in tongues. The Holy Spirit will not speak audibly through a person by force. A prophet or priest may have a message that he believes God gave him for the people. His speech is not the voice of God. It is the voice of the speaker, declaring the thoughts that he hopes to express. The utterance of an unknown tongue is God's gift of the Holy Spirit. The Holy Spirit prays on behalf of the one who is searching to please God. The person uses his or her tongue in prayer to utter an unknown language, known only to God, given by the Holy Spirit. Note that the explanation of tongues is fully revealed in Chapters 12–14 of 1 Corinthians.

Chapter 14
The Scholar

The New Testament consists of thirty-five Gospels. John wrote four of the Gospels. Luke and Peter each wrote two. Matthew and Mark each wrote one. Saul wrote twenty-four of the Gospels besides being one of the most prominent persons in the Books of Acts, written by the physician, Doctor Luke.

Saul was indeed the scholar of the New Testament. Jesus had said, "These signs will accompany those who believe: in my name . . . they will lay their hands on the sick, and they will recover" (Mark 16:17–18). Saul practiced this truth. Wherever he went people were healed, as Saul prayed for them.

The Long-Winded Scholar

Saul, like many scholars, could be long-winded. In a third-floor room, a number of people gathered to hear Saul speak. His prolonged message began in the light of day and continued into the night. The room was filled with people, and a young man had to sit on the windowsill. At midnight, the young man sank into a deep sleep. That did not trouble Saul; he kept on talking. Overcome by sleep, the young man fell out the window from the third floor to his death. Saul embraced the boy, and life returned. The boy, alive and normal, went home (Acts 20:7–12).

Bad Things Happen

Saul had no enemies, except for his former religious organization that once occupied his life. Now that he no longer belonged, his life became worthless to the people he once loved. The people used every skill to purge, kill, or otherwise, get rid of such individuals as Saul. Through their political cunning, as with Christ, Saul also met tragic penalty, due to religious bigotry.

Power to dominate the lives of others is essential for good, but also bad when used selfishly. God does not dominate a person's life. As our creator, God has the right to dominate, yet he does not. God offers everlasting life, but Adam's nature rebels, desiring to do as he pleased. The power to dominate is the reason that few people truly follow Christ.

Jesus said, "If anyone would come after me, let him deny himself and take up his cross and follow me" (Matthew 16:24). Self-denial is an enemy of childhood. Denying opportunity that is within one's grasp is the most difficult of all human tasks.

Saul's enemies were not the ungodly. His enemies were the elders of the church who failed to appreciate ideas not sanctioned by the religious authority. It was the church leaders who angrily fought against Saul, appealing to the higher authorities of government who then arrested Saul on a deceptive charge. The governing authorities soon realized that Saul had committed no crime against the State or the people. The religious authorities became resentful and filled with anger.

Regardless of Saul's innocence, the political government had to favor the majority of people. Saul, a citizen of Rome, was placed on a ship with other prisoners. Headed for Rome, a violent storm of high winds and rain caused huge waves that slammed onto the vessel. The ship sank. Despite the loss of the ship, not a man was lost due to God's love for Saul. They were able to take refuge on a small island called Malta.

The island was the home of a few people who showed extreme kindness to the two hundred seventy-six persons who became stranded on the island. The native people had a disease, so Saul laid his hands on them in prayer, and all were healed (Acts 28:1–10). After they spent three months on the island, a ship that had landed on the island became available, and so the journey to Rome was resumed.

In Rome, Saul was favored by the guards who were responsible for their prisoner. Saul was examined by the Romans who were willing to release Saul because there was no reason for putting Saul to death. Despite being imprisoned, Saul was in his own home, but he was limited in movement by the use of chains (Acts 28:20).

Saul continually proclaimed the Gospel to all who would hear him. Saul felt that he was unworthy of the Gospel, changing his name from that of the rich King, Saul, to the simple name of Paul, meaning "little one." Now named Paul, he lived two full years in his own home chained.

One day they removed his chains, took him to a location, and had him bend over. One hard swing from the ax man, and Paul was beheaded. And so ends the story of a boy named Saul who became the "little man," Paul.

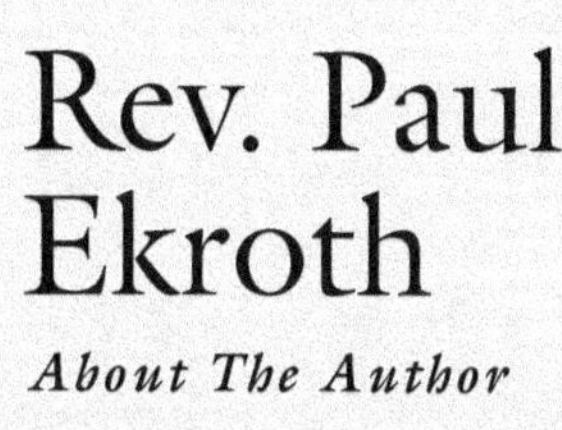

Rev. Paul Ekroth

About The Author

Rev. Paul Ekroth is a descendant of Swedish-speaking immigrants; his mother was born in Finland and his father was born in Sweden. Paul's parents immigrated to New York and finally settled in Worcester, Massachusetts, where his maternal grandfather founded and pastored two Swedish-speaking churches. Paul's dad entered one of those churches for the first time when he was 20 years old. There he heard a sermon in his native language, and he received the message of salvation and became born again.

In time, his dad met the pastor's daughter, and she eventually became his wife. Paul recalls that his dad taught him the value of hard work, and his mother taught him biblical values and how to pray.

In 1956, Paul completed four years of extensive training at the Chicago Bible College Institute where he earned an Evangelical Advanced Teacher's Certificate and Diploma of the Bible. On May 24, 1956, he was ordained as a minister of the gospel.

www.ingramcontent.com/pod-product-compliance
Lightning Source LLC
LaVergne TN
LVHW020655100826
845148LV00012B/2511

* 9 7 8 1 6 3 2 9 6 6 5 1 3 *